How to Avoid Taxes

(LEGALLY)

Discover the 7 Ways which are being used by the Wealthiest People in the World to Reduce or Eliminate their Taxes

ARX Reads

ARX READS

ARX Reads LLC

info@arxreads.com

www.arxreads.com

Table of Contents

INTRODUCTION

Imagine this, you were just hired as the president of Intel. Your starting salary is $1 million per year. You pick up the phone and call your family to give them the good news that you are finally a millionaire. Well, not so fast. With all this excitement, you forgot to consider the hard reality of making money in today's social-economic world. Which are taxes! With $1 million in earned income, you will have to pay over $300,000 in federal taxes, $29,000 in social security tax, over $100,000 in state taxes assuming you live in California, where the company headquarters is located. This means that out of your million-dollar salary, you will have to pay $468,590 in just taxes. This is over 46% of your total income going to taxes. And there is very little you can actually do to change that. And if you try to evade taxes, you can end up with a fine up to $250,000 on top of what you already. So much for being a millionaire. But wait a minute, if the IRS doesn't joke around with their taxes, why do we keep hearing about wealthy people and companies not paying theirs. This got me curious. What are these guys do differently to avoid taxes without any consequences from the IRS? Well, it turns out the tax code can be a little complicated and some of the wealthiest people in the world found a few loopholes to keep their money away from Uncle Sam's pockets. One of the simplest, yet fastest way to start saving money in taxes if you already have a good business is to turn your sole proprietor business to a corporation because these two are taxed very differently. When a person does business as a sole proprietor, they are combining their own personal finances with their business finances and their business income will be taxed, just like earned income, which can go up to 37% just for federal taxes alone.

1. Build a Corporation

If you made a million dollars a year as a sole proprietor, you will be on the hook to pay up to $370,000 in just federal taxes. But if you are a corporation, you will only have to pay $210,000 in federal taxes. Since the corporate tax rate in the US is 21%. Becoming a corporation will automatically save you $160,000 in federal taxes for that million-dollar year. And this number used to be higher in Trump's presidency. Corporate taxes went from 35% down to 21% with the tax cuts and jobs act of 2017. The only downside here is that since the corporation is a different entity than the owner, technically you don't own that money. The corporation owns the money and you own the corporation. And if you want to move the money from the company's bank account into your own bank account, by paying yourself dividends, you will have to pay an additional 15% to 20% dividend distribution tax. In some cases, this double taxation still ends up being less than if you were to pay earned income tax. Many people, even celebrities are beginning to use corporations to run their businesses. Celebrities like JC have corporations that hold the rights to the performer, which is himself. This way, the money doesn't go straight to his bank account triggering the higher tax. But rather to his corporation, JC incorporated. This not only allows the owner to take advantage of corporate tax rates but also to claim any expenses related to the business as a corporate loss. Many successful corporate owners buy their luxuries like a nice car or lease a beautiful house as long as it's related to business, which allows them to claim those purchases as a business expense, which lowers the taxable income of the company, lowering their tax bill. In a sense, they are allowed to spend money that is related to their business first, before the IRS comes to claim their share. This is an easy way for anyone with a good business to reduce their taxes, but not eliminate them.

2. Tax Havens

There are a few other loopholes, the wealthy use that allows them to not pay any taxes if they don't want to. A very common practice of multibillion-dollar companies is that use water called tax havens. These little handy loopholes are companies that are placed in offshore countries to offer these corporations and individuals, little to no tax liability and legally they can share no financial information about the company to foreign tax authorities like the US. Some tax havens are places like The Bahamas, Bermuda, Jersey and the Cayman Islands. Just to name a few. Now companies can't just send their money to a bank account to The

Bahamas to avoid taxes. There has to be a legal structure that takes advantage of the current tax laws to pretend like they made less money than they actually did. For example, let's say that you built a company and you made $100 million in profits this year. This means that in the US you will have to pay $21 million in corporate taxes based on the 21% tax rate. But what, if you can tell the government that you only made $20 million instead of a hundred, this means that you would only have to pay $4.2 million in corporate taxes instead of the normal $21 million. But how do you do that? The way many companies can legally do this is by creating a company offshore like in The Bahamas and transferred the ownership of their patents, trademarks, and intellectual property from the real company in the US to their other company in The Bahamas. And when Uncle Sam comes to collect $21 million, you can just say, sorry, we have to pay $80 million to this other company in The Bahamas to license their patents. And now they have successfully sheltered $80 million offshore and paid $0 in taxes for them because The Bahamas happens to have a 0% corporate tax rate. And instead of paying $21 million, the only paid $4.2 million. Saving around $16.8 million in taxes. This means than instead of paying 21% taxes, the only paid 4.2% of their total profits. This strategy may save lots of money in taxes, but it also has its flaws. Well, this money is hidden offshore. It cannot be used. If the company tries to bring the money back to the US, it would be taxed. This is what originally created Apple's cash problem. They had lots of money in the bank, but it was out of reach because bringing the money back would mean paying the taxes they were avoiding in the first place. So, what would it be the purpose of hiding money offshore? If you can't use it? Well, companies sheltered their money offshore to be brought back when an opportunity to save in taxes comes to light. And this happened in January of 2018, where the corporate tax rate changed from 35% to 21%. Given the perfect opportunity for companies to bring back their money and pay less and taxes. If you paid attention in the news over the last year, Apple has been aggressively bringing back their money and buying back their shares, which in term makes them more money by increasing the price of the shares, which can allow them to save in taxes in a different way.

3. Stock Options

See many company executives prefer to get paid a portion of their compensation in stock options. As the company valuation goes up, companies can create new shares to pay their executives. This creates a couple of benefits.

The executive won't pay any taxes on their compensation until they sell their stock, which puts them in control of when they are taxed.

The company can report losses in form of salaries without actually losing cash. Since they can just create new shares, they can legally report the loss, but not lose the cash. In essence, they are printing their own money in form of shares to pay their executives.

4. Using Debt

Now getting paid in shares can also create another loophole for company executives to avoid taxes. They get paid in shares. The executives can use those shares to purchase stock options, which can be used to borrow money from an investment bank while using their shares as collateral. This allows them to bypass the capital gains tax, given them free money that they can either repay later from their profits of using the money or handing over the shares themselves, given them tax-free money. A good example of this is Elon Musk. In 2017, he used about 40% of his own personal shares in Tesla as collateral for loans, which at the time was amounted to over $4 billion in Tesla shares used as collateral. In 2019, he reportedly owes over $500 million backed by his ownership in Tesla. It is unclear why he used the money for, but many say that he used this money to invest in his other companies.

5. Shell Companies

A very interesting trick that many of the corporations use is the use of shell companies, which are companies that do not have a physical location, don't have any products or any employees but are used to hold bank accounts where money can pass through to avoid being taxed. A good example of this is the company Apple, Apple reportedly had around $285 billion hidden offshore. As an American company that does business internationally, Apple would have to pay US taxes from the money that was made in other countries. Since the US is the only country that taxes based on citizenship, the company would have to pay the taxes from the country it operates in and the rest would be paid to the US in order to complete the 21%. But when there are a will and billions of dollars at stake, there's a way. Apple decided to create a company in Ireland where corporate taxes are 12.5%. Then they create another company in the Netherlands. And lastly, they have another company in Ireland that has a legal residency in Jersey, on an island off the coast of France that you guessed, it has no corporate taxes. So the company in Jersey who owns all the patents and all the intellectual property licenses the properties to the company in the Netherlands which is more of a bank account than a company. This company in the Netherlands subleases the property to the company in Ireland, which is the company that takes care of its international operations. This means that when someone buys a knife in Europe, the money goes through the Irish company that takes care of the operations. This money briefly flashes in a Dutch bank account before retiring back in Ireland. Since the company is legally registered in Jersey, it cannot be taxed. And that is how a shell company without a physical location or even any employees were used to transfer money tax-free.

6. Death Tax

Now, believe it or not, many countries will tax someone when they pass away. This is what it's called the state tax, the death tax, or the inheritance tax. Many wealthy people also call it a voluntary tax because there are a few ways to easily avoid it. One of the most popular ones is by using what it's called a GRAT (Grantor Retained Annuity Trust). This is basically a trust fund that creates an irrevocable trust for a period of time, which pays annuities. And once the trust expires the beneficiary receives all the assets tax-free.

7. Capital Gains Tax

Now, something that many wealthy people do is reinvest their money back into investments to avoid the capital gains tax. For example, let's say that you sold a few real estate properties worth $500,000. You could either pay the 20% capital gains tax or use this cash to reinvest in more property, which allows you to grow your net worth tax-free. This is where many wealthy individuals do to create massive wealth for avoiding large tax liabilities. They say that we use these $500,000 to buy five more properties, worth half a million dollars each. And let's say that in 30 years, these properties are paid off and have an appreciated value of $4 million. And the meantime you will only pay taxes on the passive income that your property generates, which is usually between 15 and 20%. While taking advantage of these tax laws, it benefits real estates such as depreciation and mortgage interest. In the end, you could use GRAT that we explained earlier to transfer your wealth to your kids tax-free.

A Gift

I have a surprise gift for you. At ARX Reads, we make smart and easy explainer eBooks on topics such as Business and Money, Computer and Internet, How to's and Advice, Etc. So, because you have bought this book of ours, we are giving away our 8 bestselling eBooks (normally $18) absolutely FREE!

GOTO – **arxreads.com/gift** and grab yours now!

I hope you found this book helpful and if you did, we'd love for you to share your thoughts by leaving a product review on Amazon. If you have any questions you would like to ask you can reach out to us at hi@arxreads.com and I'll be sure to get back to you as soon as possible.

Thank you!

Printed in Great Britain
by Amazon

71960572R00020